What Does It Mean to Be an Entrepreneur?

Young Adult Library of Small Business and Finance

Building a Business in the Virtual World

Business & Ethics

Business & the Government: Law and Taxes

Business Funding & Finances

Keeping Your Business Organized: Time Management & Workflow

Managing Employees

Marketing Your Business

Starting a Business: Creating a Plan

Understanding Business Math & Budgets

What Does It Mean to Be an Entrepreneur?

Young Adult Library of Small Business and Finance

What Does It Mean to Be an Entrepreneur?

C.F. Earl

JOHNSON PUBLIC LIBRARY
274 MAIN STREET
HACKENSACK, NJ 07601
201-343-4169

Mason Crest

Mason Crest
450 Parkway Drive, Suite D
Broomall, PA 19008
www.masoncrest.com

Copyright © 2014 by Mason Crest, an imprint of National Highlights, Inc. All rights reserved. No part of this publication may be reproduced or transmitted in any form or by any means, electronic or mechanical, including photocopying, recording, taping or any information storage and retrieval system, without permission from the publisher.

Printed in the United States of America.

First printing
9 8 7 6 5 4 3 2 1

Series ISBN: 978-1-4222-2912-5
Hardcover ISBN: 978-1-4222-2922-4
Paperback ISBN: 978-1-4222-2985-9
ebook ISBN: 978-1-4222-8912-9

The Library of Congress has cataloged the
hardcopy format(s) as follows:

    Library of Congress Cataloging-in-Publication Data

Earl, C. F.
  What does it mean to be an entrepreneur? / C.F. Earl.
    pages cm. – (Young adult library of small business and finance)
  Audience: Age 12.
  Audience: Grade 7 to 8.
   ISBN 978-1-4222-2922-4 (hardcover) – ISBN 978-1-4222-2912-5 (series) – ISBN 978-1-4222-2985-9 (pbk.) – ISBN 978-1-4222-8912-9 (ebook)
  1. Entrepreneurship–Juvenile literature. 2. New business enterprises–Management–Juvenile literature. 3. Small business–Management–Juvenile literature. I. Title.
  HB615.E267 2014
  658.1'1–dc23
                                      2013016933

Produced by Vestal Creative Services.
www.vestalcreative.com

CONTENTS

Introduction	6
1. What Does an Entrepreneur Do?	11
2. What Does It Take to Be an Entrepreneur?	21
3. Can Kids Be Entrepreneurs?	31
4. Examples of Young Entrepreneurs	39
Find Out More	60
Vocabulary	61
Index	63
About the Author and Consultant and Picture Credits	64

INTRODUCTION

Brigitte Madrian, PhD

Small businesses serve a dual role in our economy. They are the bedrock of community life in the United States, providing goods and services that we rely on day in and day out. Restaurants, dry cleaners, car repair shops, plumbers, painters, landscapers, hair salons, dance studios, and veterinary clinics are only a few of the many different types of local small business that are part of our daily lives. Small businesses are also important contributors to the engines of economic growth and innovation. Many of the successful companies that we admire today started as small businesses run out of bedrooms and garages, including Microsoft, Apple, Dell, and Facebook, to name only a few. Moreover, the founders of these companies were all very young when they started their firms. Great business ideas can come from people of any age. If you have a great idea, perhaps you would like to start your own small business. If so, you may be wondering: What does it take to start a business? And how can I make my business succeed?

A successful small business rests first and foremost on a great idea—a product or service that other people or businesses want and are willing to pay for. But a good idea is not enough. Successful businesses start with a plan. A business plan defines what the business will do, who its customers will be, where the firm will be located, how the firm will market the company's product, who the firm will hire, how the business will be financed, and what, if any, are the firm's plans for future growth. If a firm needs a loan from a bank in order to start up, the bank will mostly likely want to see a written business plan. Writing a business plan helps an entrepreneur think

through all the possible road blocks that could keep a business from succeeding and can help convince a bank to make a loan to the firm.

Once a firm has the funding in place to open shop, the next challenge is to connect with the firm's potential customers. How will potential customers know that the company exists? And how will the firm convince these customers to purchase the company's product? In addition to finding customers, most successful businesses, even small ones, must also find employees. What types of employees should a firm hire? And how much should they be paid? How do you motivate employees to do their jobs well? And what do you do if employees don't get along? Managing employees is an important skill in running almost any successful small business.

Finally, firms must also understand the rules and regulations that govern how they operate their business. Some rules, like paying taxes, apply to all businesses. Other rules apply to only certain types of firms. Does the firm need a license to operate? Are there restrictions on where the firm can locate or when it can be open? What other regulations must the firm comply with?

Starting up a small business is a lot of work. But despite the hard work, most small business owners find their jobs

What Does It Mean to Be an Entrepreneur?

rewarding. While many small business owners are happy to have their business stay small, some go on to grow their firms into more than they ever imagined, big companies that service customers throughout the world.

What will your small business do?

Brigitte Madrian, PhD
Aetna Professor of Public Policy and Corporate Management
Harvard Kennedy School

Introduction

ONE

What Does an Entrepreneur Do?

If you've ever thought about starting a business, or have even already started one, you may be an entrepreneur and not even know it. Entrepreneur is a fancy word for a risk-taker in business.

Not many people say they want to be entrepreneurs when they grow up, but plenty of people end up as entrepreneurs. When you think about it, though, it's a pretty good goal to *aspire* to. However, you don't even have to wait until you're older and out of school to be an entrepreneur. In fact, young people often

If you're good at organizing people and you have a good idea for making the world a better place, you might want to try your hand at being a social entrepreneur.

make some of the best entrepreneurs. You might be the next big entrepreneur yourself!

A Certain Kind of Risk

Not all risk-takers are entrepreneurs. People who mountain bike or rock climb are risk-takers, but they aren't entrepreneurs. In general, people who take physical risks aren't considered to be entrepreneurs.

People who take risks to start businesses are entrepreneurs. The risk might be that they don't have much money, but they're going to set up a business anyway. Businesses often take a lot of money to get started. Entrepreneurs could lose all their money if the business doesn't work out.

Not all business risks have to do with money. The risk might be that no one has ever heard of the technology an entrepreneur created and now wants to sell; maybe no one will want the technology. Another risk entrepreneurs take is giving up time they might have spent on other things they enjoy. An entrepreneur may have to dedicate a lot of hours to make her business successful. She may not get to spend time with friends and family, relax, or work at another job.

Entrepreneurs don't necessarily have to start a business. They could also start a **nonprofit** or a community project. However, people are usually talking about business when they talk about entrepreneurs.

SOCIAL ENTREPRENEURS

Not all entrepreneurs are business people. Some are more concerned with taking risks that make the world a better place; they're called social entrepreneurs. They think they have good answers that solve social problems like poverty, hunger, and violence. With their ideas, they can make big changes, so they are willing to take on the risks involved. Social entrepreneurs set up nonprofits, work for universities or the government, or start social movements. They are some of the leaders of social change around the world.

Why?

Entrepreneurs usually like what they do. They think it's fun! They like the feeling of starting new businesses and taking risks. It gives them a thrill. They also like the happiness and excitement that comes with overcoming challenges and succeeding.

Many entrepreneurs also want to make money. They think they have a great idea to make a lot of money, and they are willing to take risks to do it. Entrepreneurs who are successful can make millions and millions of dollars. Of course, plenty of entrepreneurs never get that far.

Entrepreneurs may also want to make the world better. They see a problem that needs to be solved, and they think they have

ENTREPRENEURIAL SKILLS

Being entrepreneur takes more than just be willing to take risks. Entrepreneurs need to be creative. They have to come up with new products and services to sell, as well as advertisements and more. Getting along with people is also important when it comes to business. Entrepreneurs need to be able to get along with customers, employees, and investors. Another skill entrpreneurs need is organization. Businesses have a lot going on, and they need to be able to keep track of everything. Receipts, customer orders, and budgets are just some of the things they'll need to keep organized.

What Does It Mean to Be an Entrepreneur?

Entrepreneurs want to make money—and they have good ideas for doing that.

What Does an Entrepreneur Do?

15

A graphic representation of the steps a business plans to take.

the business to fix it. When an entrepreneur successfully sets up a business, he feels good that he added something valuable to the world.

Steps

Entrepreneurs go through several steps before they start businesses. Although they like taking on risk, they don't just jump into a business or project without any thought!

First, entrepreneurs look for opportunities. They look for problems people have, or things people need or want. Then they look around and see if anyone is trying to solve those problems already. If not, then they have the beginning of a business idea!

What Does It Mean to Be an Entrepreneur?

Next, entrepreneurs will figure out some ideas about how to solve that problem or fill that need. They might come up with several ideas at once. Then they can think about all of them and see if any are worth building a business around. Some ideas might not really work in real life, but some might be great business ideas.

After an entrepreneur picks a business idea, she can start planning. Starting a business is a big deal. You need to think through a business before you start. Entrepreneurs ask themselves a lot of questions before they start a business, and they try to come up with good answers. Most entrepreneurs will create a business plan at this point, which outlines exactly what their business will be like.

Once the business is all planned, the entrepreneur needs to raise money! He'll need money for developing and making the product or service, advertising, buying equipment, and more. Bigger businesses need lots of money, while smaller businesses need less.

This is where entrepreneurship really comes in. An entrepreneur has to be really good at convincing people to give her money so she can make her idea reality. She may try to get people to *invest* in her business. She might apply for *loans* from banks or apply for *grants* from the government or other businesses. All that money will add up if an entrepreneur is really good at convincing people her idea is good.

Once the entrepreneur has the money, he can start the business. Often, new businesses run by entrepreneurs are called startups. At first, the startup is small, but if the entrepreneur is a good businessperson, it will grow fast.

As the business grows (or fails), the entrepreneur often moves on. Entrepreneurs like the challenge of starting businesses and helping them grow. As soon as a business looks stable and like it will survive, many entrepreneurs hand over control to someone else and move on to the next project.

What Does an Entrepreneur Do?

BUSINESS PLANS

An entrepreneur needs a plan. Every business needs a map of where it's going, and how it will get there. That map is called a business plan. A good business plan should include:

- a description of the business, along with its goals and the reasons why it exists.
- a marketing plan, which describes how the business will get customers to buy what it's selling. Marketing includes advertising, packaging, and places where the business will sell its goods or services.
- a description of the competition.
- a section on how the business will organize and manage itself, including any employees it will hire.
- a description of what the busines is selling. This could be products (things for sale) or services (things people will pay the business to do).
- a financial plan, covering how the business will get the money it needs and how much profit it hopes to make.

If you're an entrepreneur, you should have a hard copy of your business plan on paper so you can look at it easily. You should also have a computer file, so you can easily change and update your business plan when you need to.

Entrepreneurs versus Small Business Owners

You might be wondering how an entrepreneur is different from anyone else who starts a business. In many cases, they are the same thing. Entrepreneurs and people who start businesses are interested in solving problems and making money.

However, there are sometimes a few differences. Entrepreneurs tend to focus on the ideas behind the business. They come up with good ideas, get money, and then start a business. Then they may leave to do something else. Small business owners are more often interested in sticking with their business. They also have a good business idea, but they want to run their businesses and see them grow. They are less likely to move on, unless their businesses don't succeed.

Business owners are managers. They like to organize the business and be the boss. Entrepreneurs are often more focused on the ideas and set up. They probably aren't all that interested in actually running the business. They're idea people!

TWO

What Does It Take to Be an Entrepreneur?

People argue about whether entrepreneurs are born or made. Some people think that only those individuals born with certain personalities will become entrepreneurs. Others think you can learn how to be an entrepreneur.

The truth is that either is possible. Some people are born with a talent for coming up with creative ideas and a **passion** for making them happen. Other people figure out over time that they want to be entrepreneurs, and they learn how to make that happen.

So what does it take to be an entrepreneur? No matter if they are born or made, or a little of both, entrepreneurs tend to have some things in common.

If you recognize some of the following qualities in yourself, you might be a great **candidate** for becoming an entrepreneur. Or maybe you already are one. Then these qualities won't come as any surprise.

Scientific Studies on Entrepreneurship

Scientists have been studying whether someone has to be born an entrepreneur to actually be one. Some scientists have done studies on twins. If entrepreneurship was *genetic* only, identical twins, who have the same DNA, would either both be entrepreneurs or both not be entrepreneurs. If one twin ends up being an entrepreneur and the other doesn't, then scientists can tell that at least some people learn how to be entrepreneurs. The scientific studies showed that entrepreneurship is about half—48 percent—genetic and half learned.

Creativity

Creativity is really important in entrepreneurship. No, entrepreneurs don't have to be artists or musicians. But they do have to be able to think "outside the box." An entrepreneur should be able to notice problems and find creative solutions to them.

Instead of art, entrepreneurs create businesses. They create products and services people will want to buy. Then they create an entire business to sell those products and services.

What Does It Mean to Be an Entrepreneur?

Entrepreneurs also have to be creative in how they handle problems in their businesses. Setting up a business never goes perfectly. An entrepreneur might run into problems getting enough money. Or people might not think her idea is good. Or she might not hire the right people to work for her new companies. Entrepreneurs always run into problems of some sort.

But problems don't stand in an entrepreneur's way. She can figure out how to get around the problem. She can find new ways to raise money. Or find a new way to talk about her idea (or even change the idea a little).

Persistence

Entrepreneurs are nothing if not persistent. They never give up, and they always work hard. They are determined to succeed.

Problems and setbacks don't worry entrepreneurs. In fact, some of them like setbacks because that means they have a puzzle to solve. Other people might quit if they suddenly lost a lot of money they were counting on to start their business. But a true entrepreneur will refuse to give up. He'll simply find the money somewhere else without panicking.

Independence

Entrepreneurs don't usually want to work for other people. They want to be their own bosses, make their own hours, and choose their own work.

Independent people can make decisions on their own, without needing other people for direction. That's exactly what entrepreneurs do, though successful entrepreneurs can also listen to other people's input.

Sometimes entrepreneurs can be TOO independent. They want to do everything, and they won't let other people help. Being too independent can get in the way of making a business successful, once other people start working with the entrepreneur.

Passion

Entrepreneurs are just plain happy being entrepreneurs. If you really enjoy doing entrepreneurial things like creating business ideas, and telling other people all about them, then you're probably an entrepreneur! If you are happier working as an employee for someone else, then you are probably not an entrepreneur.

People can be passionate about a lot of things, like traveling, cooking, or sports. Entrepreneurs are passionate about solving problems with new ideas and turning them into businesses. And when an entrepreneur comes up with a new idea, he is really passionate about making it work. He'll do just about anything possible to make it work.

All this passion requires a lot of energy. Many entrepreneurs work around the clock on their business ideas. Entrepreneurs know they need a lot of energy to succeed, so they don't mind working so hard. Other people might worry about them, because some entrepreneurs forget to eat, sleep, or relax while they are working on a business. You won't often find entrepreneurs in front of the TV or taking a nap.

People Skills

Although entrepreneurs are independent, they do have to work with other people. They need to talk to people about giving them money. They have to spread the word about their businesses so they can get customers. They may have to hire employees to work at their businesses.

Entrepreneurs should have good people skills, which means several things. Good people skills include being able to communicate with people well. They don't want to offend people or not get the right information across if they are trying to tell someone about their businesses!

LEADERSHIP

Leaders are people who organize other to get a job done. Leaders work in the government, at schools, in social movements, and in businesses. Some of the most visible business leaders are entrepreneurs. They organize lots of people to start up businesses—that's basically their job description! Leaders don't have to be entrepreneurs. They could be employees that work at a company, or business owners who step in after an entrepreneur leaves. But all entrepreneurs are leaders.

Do you have good ideas? Do you have enough self-confidence to make those ideas reality? If so, you might make a good entrepreneur!

   Really good people skills also means being able to inspire others. Good entrepreneurs are likable and friendly, and they can convince people to follow them. They can get people excited about their ideas—and ready to work hard for those ideas.

26   **What Does It Mean to Be an Entrepreneur?**

Self-Confidence

Entrepreneurs tend to have a lot of confidence in their ideas and their abilities. Lots of self-confidence is how they can make decisions and get so passionate about ideas. They don't second guess themselves, and they believe they have the skills and knowledge to turn their ideas into businesses. Entrepreneurs' confidence convinces other people that their ideas are great too.

Many people do not have self-confidence. They think that nothing they do will be good enough, or that they are not smart enough or good enough at talking to people. Not having self-confidence gets in the way of taking action and making decisions. Entrepreneurs aren't necessarily better at doing things than other people. They just have enough self-confidence to do them.

Good entrepreneurs have the right amount of confidence. Entrepreneurs with too much self-confidence will take risks they shouldn't. They'll think they can do anything, and may not plan in advance. Entrepreneurs who take too many bad risks and have too much confidence won't run successful businesses.

Types of Entrepreneurs

Not all entrepreneurs are exactly the same. People have different personalities and ways of working. They also have different circumstances.

One kind of entrepreneur starts out knowing she wants to be an entrepreneur. Her dream is to come up with an idea and then start a business. This kind of entrepreneur starts from scratch, and probably already has the personality traits of an entrepreneur.

Other people will come up with an idea and may not really be sure what they want to do with it. They are scientists who have done some research. Or they are students who have studied a problem. Or just normal people who solve a problem or invent something.

Those sorts of people don't set out to be entrepreneurs. They just stumble upon an answer to a problem. Then they realize they could make a business out of it, while helping lots of people solve the same problem. You could call them accidental entrepreneurs. They might have some entrepreneurial skills and qualities before, which inspire them to turn their idea into a business. But they also learn about entrepreneurship along the way.

Are You an Entrepreneur?

An article on Forbes.com lists several questions you can ask yourself to get a better idea whether you are an entrepreneur:

- Do you know a lot about your business's **industry**?
- Do you have a good idea of what your business's future looks like?
- Do you have a history of successful ideas?
- Are you smart and curious?
- Can you identify and manage business risk?
- Do you have **charisma**, **integrity**, and the ability to attract talented employees to your business?

You have to be able to convince investors that the answer to these questions is yes. If you think this describes you—or might describe you after you have some more experience—then entrepreneurship might be right for you!

What Does It Mean to Be an Entrepreneur?

WHAT DOES MONEY HAVE TO DO WITH IT?

Lots of people think entrepreneurs have to really want to be rich to do what they do. Most people wouldn't mind making a lot of money and being rich, and entrepreneurs are no exception. However, entrepreneurs almost always have more goals than making money. They really want to solve problems and start businesses. If they make a lot of money along the way, that's a bonus!

You don't have to have business experience to see yourself as an entrepreneur. You may have started a **campaign** in your school to save your orchestra, which was going to be cut. Or you may have organized a fundraiser for someone who lost his home in a fire. If you've had a good idea and then organized others to make your idea reality, you may have what it takes to be an entrepreneur.

Maybe you have already started a business, or are thinking about it. Not everyone with a business idea is an entrepreneur. You have to actually turn your idea into reality. If you have done that, then congratulations—you can consider yourself an entrepreneur!

THREE

Can Kids Be Entrepreneurs?

Some jobs need a lot of training to do. You won't become a physicist by the time you've finished high school, or a doctor. You have to have years of special education before you can get those jobs. You can, however, become an entrepreneur at just about any age.

Many entrepreneurs are adults, but plenty are teenagers or even kids. Entrepreneurs don't let age stop them in their quest to make ideas happen!

Experience Matters...Sort Of

Experience helps when it comes to entrepreneurship. Knowing a little bit about what businesses do, how people raise money for businesses, and how they find customers are all pretty helpful when it comes to starting your own business.

One study showed that 87 percent of successful entrepreneurs started businesses that were related to their previous experiences. They didn't just start up a business they knew nothing about. They used what they already knew to start a new business.

BUSINESS IDEAS

If you want to start your own business and try out being an entrepreneur, here are some ideas. There are lots more out there!

- Babysitting or pet sitting.
- Lawn care (landscaping, mowing lawns, shoveling snow, raking leaves).
- Blogging, which can make money through advertisements.
- Dog walking.
- Jewelry making.
- Knitting or sewing clothes.
- Making prepared foods such as jam or baked goods.
- Graphic design for websites or advertisements.
- Developing a game or other application for computers or smartphones.

What Does It Mean to Be an Entrepreneur?

Another study showed that the average age of entrepreneurs is about forty. These entrepreneurs have worked in companies for fifteen or twenty years, and they've learned a lot. They learn how to **manage** a company. They learn how to market and how to create products and services. Then they use what they have learned to start their own businesses.

You actually might have more experience than you think you do, though. You don't need experience running a business or working at a company. Doing school projects, for example, can be good entrepreneurial experience. When you get to design and work on your own project and then present it to your class, you are practicing entrepreneurship.

And sometimes, lots of experience just doesn't matter too much. Some young people can turn their ideas into businesses without much trouble. Either they want to start a business, or they accidentally come up with a business.

If you really want to be an entrepreneur, don't let a lack of experience stop you! Think about all the things you've already done and figure out what you've already learned about entrepreneurship. If you've ever watched TV or gone online (and who hasn't?), you already know about advertising. If you've ever fundraised for a sports team or class at school, you know something about how to raise money. Starting a business might not be such a stretch if you think about all the ways in which you've already had some practice.

Kids Are Better Entrepreneurs

Some people even think young people are better entrepreneurs than adults. Many kids and teenagers have some skills that adults don't. Young people are often more willing to try new things and

Some schools offer classes that teach young adults business skills. Working together as a team is an important part of the classes.

take risks. Since that is one of the most important things an entrepreneur can do, it makes sense that young people would be good entrepreneurs.

Some people also say that young people have more energy than many adults. Young adults can stay up late, working on business projects. (Of course, schoolwork has to be done, so young people can't spend ALL their time being entrepreneurs.) They're less likely to tire out when faced with problems and obstacles.

Even a lack of experience can give kids an advantage when it comes to entrepreneurship. Adults already have ideas about

What Does It Mean to Be an Entrepreneur?

how business should work. Young people who don't have much work experience don't have those same ideas—and this can actuall work to their advantage. They are free to think up new ways of doing business, which might work better than what people are doing now. When you're young is the right time to try out being an entrepreneur!

Learning Entrepreneurship

You may want to be an entrepreneur, but you're not sure where to start. There are plenty of places you can learn.

ENTREPRENEURSHIP CLASS

In North and South Dakota, several schools are adding entrepreneurship classes to the school day. The classes are meant to teach students about the basics of entrepreneurship, and also to encourage them to start their own businesses. Many young people leave their hometowns in the Dakotas because they can't find jobs. Entrepreneurship classes are teaching them they can make their own jobs! More recent graduates might choose to stay in their hometowns if they can start businesses of their own. In one class, students learned how to write business plans. In another, they played a computer game in which they were the owners of convenience stores. The decisions they made affected how well their businesses did.

Can Kids Be Entrepreneurs?

This young person is already getting entrepreneurial experience. All it takes is some vegetables, some lemonade, a stand—and an enterprising spirit!

What Does It Mean to Be an Entrepreneur?

As a young person, you're used to learning new things. You learn math and science and writing all the time. Even if you're not really excited about any of those things, you're used to learning new things and practicing new skills.

Just like with math and writing, you can learn about entrepreneurship. Some high schools offer classes. So do local **community colleges** or education centers.

You can also learn about entrepreneurship by doing it! If you want to be an entrepreneur, but you aren't sure exactly how to make it happen, do some research. Then start your own business. You'll probably make some mistakes along the way, but that's okay. You won't get very far if you don't try.

Maybe your very first attempt at being an entrepreneur will succeed. Even if you don't succeed, you will have learned a lot along the way. If you are a true entrepreneur, you will try again and again, always learning along the way. Then someday you'll succeed.

Perhaps the best way to learn about entrepreneurship as a young person is to look at the examples of other kids and teens who have started their own businesses. They haven't let their age stop them, and they have set up some pretty successful **ventures**.

Can Kids Be Entrepreneurs?

FOUR

Examples of Young Entrepreneurs

All over the country and the world, there are examples of young entrepreneurs. Not every young person who sets out to create his own business succeeds. But the ones who do get a lot of attention. Here are some of them. As you'll see, they all reached success through different paths.

Adam Horwitz with Aaron Darko, another young entrepreneur. You can check out Aaron's story online at millionaireat24.com.

Adam Horwitz

As a teenager, Adam Horwitz tried out lots of business ideas. When he was fifteen, he started a website that listed parties and other events in Los Angeles, where he lived. He wasn't setting up a business, but he was already using entrepreneurial skills. His idea was TOO good, though. Hundreds of people visited the website and went to the parties. Adam ended up shutting the website down because too many people would show up at an event.

He later tried out several other ideas, with the focus on making money. Eventually, Adam came up with a successful website

What Does It Mean to Be an Entrepreneur?

Dude I Hate My Job – <u>Anything Is Possible</u>

DudeIHateMyJob.com

One of Adam's latest ventures is this training course that shows readers how to generate income by blogging about the things they love.

Examples of Young Entrepreneurs

Adam works hard, and has fun along the way. You can find out more about him online at www.dudeihatemyjob.com/affiliates.php.

 42   **What Does It Mean to Be an Entrepreneur?**

selling online courses about how to make money online. He went on to create several more very successful online businesses.

As a young person, Adam understands how important the Internet is to business. He says, "It's also so easy to get your opinion and to get your ideas out to the world, unlike having to hand out business cards and having to go talk to people personally. With the Internet, you can put up a video on YouTube and potentially everyone in the world can watch that video if they decided to watch it and if they had Internet access." Adam has made all of his money with Internet businesses.

Over time, Adam got better and better at business. He made a lot of mistakes at first, because it was his first time being a business entrepreneur. For example, he struggled to get enough people to learn about and support his first business.

When he went to create another business, it was lot easier for him. He explains, "It was twenty times easier, because first of all you've done it before, so you kind of can look back at what you did on the first one…you have more insight and you have a better understanding of what to do next." He knew more about what he was doing, and he also had a lot of **contacts**. He adds, "On top of that you have a huge e-mail list—or a pretty big e-mail list, at least."

Adam has been successful partly because he hasn't been afraid of tackling new opportunities. He is a classic entrepreneur. He has a lot to say about taking chances and never giving up. In one interview, he says, "If everything completely fails, you're still at school. You're still going to get your degree. So, it doesn't matter as long as you have fun doing it, work your way up, and stay dedicated. There's no real loss. Enjoy the way up." He learns along the way and refuses to give up, even when his business ideas fail. In the end, because he didn't give up, he figured out how to run businesses successfully and made a lot of money.

Examples of Young Entrepreneurs

Adam encourages other young business people to never give up. His advice is: "Don't listen to what other people say. If you're a young entrepreneur and you're trying to make it big online, don't think that you can't do it. With the Internet the way it is now, you can do anything. Even if everyone is saying, 'No—it will never happen. Everything online is a scam!' . . . Check them out of your mind and go for it. That's what I did and I'm doing well, I think." Adam followed his passion and ended up with a successful business.

Adam, like a lot of other young entrepreneurs struggled a little to convince other people he was serious about his businesses. He says, "Even my friends were so **stereotyped** into thinking that you can't do anything when you're young—that you have to wait until you're older and have a degree to actually become successful. So, whenever I would tell people, 'I'm doing this,' they wouldn't take it seriously." Adam didn't listen to his friends or other people who discouraged him, though. He kept going.

He looked on the bright side of things. "Age also has its benefits," he says. "For instance, I use my age as a marketing advantage. I can target younger people. I'm eighteen years old. I say, 'If I'm eighteen years old, you could be doing the same thing no matter how old you are.'" Instead of getting frustrated about his age, he used it to find new opportunities and made other young people into customers.

Leanna Archer

Leanna Archer was just nine when she started her hair-care product business that is still going strong today. Leanna is an example of an entrepreneur who stumbled on a business almost by accident.

When she first started out, Leanna gave her friends little samples of the hair product she made, which was originally made by her grandmother. "The next thing you know," Leanna says, "we had checks coming in the mail, people at our doorstep with $20.00, asking how much of this product can I get for $20.00?" She hadn't even meant to start selling it, but her business was born.

Examples of Young Entrepreneurs

After that, Leanna **embraced** being an entrepreneur. She built up her business over time so that it now earns $100,000 a year! She has pretty impressive goals too. She says, "I hope to expand my customer base worldwide and eventually have Leanna's Hair Products sold in retail stores everywhere!"

Leanna has been featured in lots of interviews in magazines, online, and on TV. Some of the magazines she's been in include *Forbes*, *Ebony*, and *Success*. She has been interviewed on TV on NBC, ABC, BET, and FOX. She first started reaching out to the **media** when she was only nine, and she eventually got her first interview. After that, more magazines started contacting her, and more people read about her business.

Leanna had the confidence it took to tell the world about her business. For example, she tells the story of an award she applied for: "One of my most recent experiences was a global entrepreneurs award . . . for college students only. But you enter the contest and after choosing out a handful of **CEOs** and company owners, they would fly you out there and give out awards and give you **mentors** and people to talk to in how to improve your business. And I knew that it was for college students only but of course I filled out the application anyway and sent it in. And because of that, since I was in high school, the company that's been around for a couple of decades now, they decided to start a high school global entrepreneurial award just because of that."

Leanna is a business entrepreneur, but she is also a social entrepreneur. She tries to solve the social problems she sees. Recently, she has set up the Leanna Archer Education Foundation. With the money she sets aside, she builds schools in Haiti, her family's homeland. Without Leanna's leadership, the foundation wouldn't exist.

Like Adam, Leanna also felt her age had its pluses and minuses in the business world. Sometimes people wouldn't take

What Does It Mean to Be an Entrepreneur?

Leanna shares her success with her family's homeland by building schools like this one in Haiti.

her seriously because she was so young when she started her business. She would talk about her business, and adults wouldn't bother listening. Her parents were even doubtful. However, she looked on the positive side and has found that her young age has actually helped her.

"Well, the pros of my age throughout the past couple of years," Leanna says, "were when people heard that there was a hair and body care product company run by a nine-year-old; that alone caught people's attention. It made the community interested in what I was doing because entrepreneurship in young ages is pretty rare." Part of her success is exactly because she's so young!

Examples of Young Entrepreneurs

Maddie Bradshaw

Maddie Bradshaw is an extremely successful teenage entrepreneur. She is an example of an inventor entrepreneur, who came up with a product and then created a business to sell it.

At the age of ten, she invented a product called Snap Caps, a necklace made of bottle caps. At first, she made them just for her friends and family. Eventually, she took fifty of her necklaces to a local toy store. The store agreed to put them on the shelves, and within a couple hours, they were gone! In an interview, she describes her early business days by saying, "At that point, I knew I was onto something. I think we were successful in the

Maggie became a millionaire selling these necklaces.

What Does It Mean to Be an Entrepreneur?

beginning because I was more focused on having fun and less worried about failing."

Maddie knew she could make a real business out of Snap Caps. She decided to organize her business, and start making money. Maddie and her family set up M3 Girl Designs, LLC. Today, she is the president of her company. She goes to company business meetings, advertises the company at **trade shows**, and creates new products. Her little sister is the vice president. Her mother is the CEO (the chief executive officer), which makes the business easier to run because Maddie isn't eighteen yet.

Maddie knows a lot about talking to other people about her business. She is skilled in convincing people to give her money.

In 2012, Maddie appeared on the TV show *Shark Tank*. Contestants on the show have to convince five investors, called Sharks, to give them money to keep their businesses going. Although nervous, Maddie made a good presentation on *Shark Tank*. She convinced three of the Sharks to give her $300,000 in investment money! She also got some good advice from them about how to run her business.

Maddie has learned a lot about starting and running a company. She started with $300, and now makes $1.6 million a year. She wants to teach other young people how to do the same thing, so she's written a book called *You Can Start a Business, Too*. Maddie loves business and likes to teach others about it. "I love that I have an opportunity to reach out and help others," she says.

Anshul Samar

One young man who is passionate about science has turned that excitement into a business. Anshul Samar is the inventor of a chemistry board game called Elementeo. As a young teen, Anshul

spent a few years creating and developing his board game, which first started selling in 2008.

He worked long and hard on his board game, perfecting it and telling everyone he knew about what he was doing. Anshul wanted his board game to be a big deal. He didn't want just a few people playing it—he wanted the whole country playing it!

Anshul quickly realized he needed the money to match his goal. As a young person, he didn't have lots of money just lying around. "When I was in sixth grade, I applied for a grant," Anshul explains. "I didn't even ask my dad for anything. The California Association for the Gifted gave me $500. It was like my pre-, pre-**seed funding**. That $500 is what got me going for the next two years. It would have been very hard to start this without someone trusting me, a thirteen-year-old, with $500." Even from the start, Anshul was good at getting people to give his business money.

The $500 grant got Anshul started, and even kept him going for two years. After that, he realized he needed some more money to truly make his game great. He borrowed some from his dad, who is also an entrepreneur. Anshul's dad believed in his son enough that he loaned his son some money.

Anshul learned how important money is to start a business. He says, "That's actually one of my personal goals, as an entrepreneur. There are a lot of youth in the world with an idea. They don't have someone to believe in them, and they don't have the money to do it. A lot of people out there don't have encouragement. I want to give $500, $1,000, $2,000 grants to youth around the world."

When asked in an interview if he wanted to be famous, Anshul said he wasn't that excited about fame. However, he did say, "There is really only one reason I would want to be famous—being famous means that people are willing to listen to you." He went on to say, "It would be great if I could reach out to the

What Does It Mean to Be an Entrepreneur?

In 2009, Anshul received the Davidson Fellowship Award for $25,000 in Washington, D.C. He used the award to help his business grow. He got the award in the "Outside the Box" category.

Examples of Young Entrepreneurs

Zoe with one of her creations..

What Does It Mean to Be an Entrepreneur?

world and tell everybody that science is really about battling, fun, and excitement, not so much about symbols and long formulas. I would also love to tell everybody that age doesn't have an affect on entrepreneurship—don't be afraid to create an idea, combat with the obstacles, and conquer the world." Like other young entrepreneurs, he hasn't let his age stop him from being an entrepreneur.

Zoe Damacela

Zoe Damacela is another young entrepreneur who is making it big. Her fashion company, Zoe Damacela Apparel, has successfully been selling dresses and other clothes for several years. Zoe was a freshman in high school when she started her business. Pretty soon, she was selling dozens of dresses. Eventually, her business caught the eye of some big names. Zoe has appeared on *The Tyra Banks Show*, won *Seventeen* magazine's Pretty Amazing contest (and even appeared on the cover), and gave a speech at the White House.

Although Zoe has learned a lot over the years, she was a born entrepreneur. In fact, fashion design wasn't her first business. "I really wanted a Razor scooter," Zoe says. "All of my friends had one. My mom kept saying 'No. No. No. It's not your birthday.' She finally said, 'If you can raise half the money yourself I'll pay for the rest.' I think she said that just to get me to stop bothering her. I ended up making greeting cards and selling them around the neighborhood. Within a couple of hours I had enough money to buy my scooter." Zoe had business smarts even when she was eight!

By the time she was a teenager, she had saved up some money from her business adventures. Now it was time to try something even bigger. "[My mom] was very **adamant** about the fact that if

Being on the cover of a popular magazine was great publicity for Zoe's business.

54

What Does It Mean to Be an Entrepreneur?

I wanted to work and succeed, I had to do everything by myself," Zoe says.

She was about to take an even bigger business risk and spend all of the money she had saved to start a new business. She paid her business startup costs herself, with the money she had saved. She took a sewing class, and used her sewing machine and her skills to start making clothes.

The risk paid off. Zoe was good at fashion design and she had the skills to make a business work. That doesn't mean she didn't make any mistakes, though. For example, Zoe first sold her products too cheaply. She sold dresses for $13. After a little while, she realized all her hard work and her creativity made the dresses worth more than that. And it turned out that people would pay a lot more for her dresses. She now sells her dresses for hundreds or even thousands of dollars.

Today, Zoe is in college and hopes to study business. She also supports the Network for Teaching Entrepreneurship, an organization that teaches young people in poor communities about business skills like marketing and *financing*. She wants to give people the same chance she had to start their own businesses.

Food From the 'Hood

Entrepreneurs don't just work alone. Some work together in teams. An example of an entrepreneurial team is a business called Food From the 'Hood.

In 1992, people started *rioting* in Los Angeles. They were angry that white police officers had beaten a black man named Rodney King. The police officers weren't punished by the law, and people got angry and rioted. In the end, hundreds of people were hurt or killed in the riot.

Examples of Young Entrepreneurs

Urban gardens can help communities—and make money too!

Lots of people were deeply saddened by what happened. One group of high school students at Crenshaw High School in Los Angeles decided to do something to promote peace. They were upset about what was happening, and they wanted to help fix their community. They decided to turn some empty space into a garden and help feed hungry people from the food they grew. During their first few months, they figured out how to grow vegetables and donated all the food they grew to a homeless shelter.

The people who started Food From the 'Hood (FFTH) were social entrepreneurs at this point. They saw a lot of problems in their neighborhood, and they decided that a garden would help solve them.

What Does It Mean to Be an Entrepreneur?

Soon, the hunger program became a business, and the organizers became business entrepreneurs too. After first focusing on donating all the food they grew to the shelter, the Crenshaw students brought their leftovers to a local farmers' market. They sold $150 of veggies in a half an hour. They were on to a business idea!

From then on, they combined social and business entrepreneurship. Pretty much everything they did to make money also also helped the community, though. They turned unused space into beautiful gardens, which made the neighborhood nicer. They continued to donate produce to people in need. They worked toward peace in the neighborhood.

Next, Food From the 'Hood created and started selling salad dressings. The first salad dressing they made was called "Straight Out the Garden Creamy Italian Dressing." They added "No Fat Honey Mustard" two years later, and eventually Ranch dressing.

After the students figured out how to make the dressings, they had to figure out how to sell them. They marketed their products to stores in the area, and convinced many stores to put the dressing on their shelves. They also started selling the dressing on Amazon.com. After a few years of hard work, Food From the 'Hood sold salad dressing at two thousand stores and was making $250,000 a year! The company clearly knew how to market to the right people.

The company also provided employment for Crenshaw students. The business is run entirely by high school students called student managers. They do all the work, from planting the gardens, to advertising, to managing the money.

One of the business's goals is to help get student employees into college after high school. In fact, 50 percent of the **profits** Food From the 'Hood make go into a scholarship fund. (The other

Examples of Young Entrepreneurs

Crenshaw High School and the surrounding community, where FFTH has made a real difference.

50 percent is used to keep the business growing.) Each student employee ends up with between $2,000 and $3,000 to spend on college, depending on how much time and effort he or she has put in to the company. The money makes a lot of difference for students who may not otherwise be able to afford college. By 2007, the business had given out $200,000 in scholarships. Asija Chappel, a student who was part of Food From the 'Hood, says, "Food From the 'Hood is an important resource for the students involved, the school, and the community as a whole."

What Does It Mean to Be an Entrepreneur?

Terie Smith, another former employee, said, "FFTH is a business but it teaches much more. We learn how to take responsibility for our actions, how to set priorities, and how to be leaders instead of followers."

Tammy Bird, a cofounder of Food From the 'Hood says, "It's a place for them to do their homework. It's a place to do college preparatory. It's a place to do their business and pick up entrepreneurial skills."

Beyond just making money, Food From the 'Hood is working hard to improve the community. It teaches young people entrepreneurial skills like leadership—and it gives them hope for the future.

The Right Attitude

All these young people prove that you don't have to be an adult to be amazingly successful. You just need to have the right attitude, a passion for entrepreneurship and business, and a willingness to learn and take risks.

If you want to be an entrepreneur, do some more research and then work hard. Entrepreneurs who keep trying eventually create brand-new, successful businesses.

Find Out More

Online

8 Kid Entrepreneurs to Watch
money.cnn.com/galleries/2011/smallbusiness/1105/gallery.kid_entrepreneurs/index.html

BizKids
bizkids.com

Entrepreneur.com
www.entrepreneur.com

Teaching Kids Business: Entrepreneurs
www.teachingkidsbusiness.com/entrepreneurship-program.htm

In Books

Hansen, Mark Victor. *The Richest Kids in America*. Newport Beach, Calif.: Hansen House, 2009.

Mariotti, Steve. *The Young Entrepreneur's Guide to Starting and Running a Business.* New York: Three Rivers Press, 2000.

Toren, Adam and Matthew Toren. *Kidpreneurs: Young Entrepreneurs with Big Ideas!* Business Plan Media Group, 2009.

Vocabulary

Adamant: firm, unyielding.
Aspire: to want to achieve or become something.
Campaign: organized work directed toward a specific goal.
Candidate: someone who is applying for a job.
CEOs: chief executive officers are the people who manage companies.
Charisma: charm and friendliness that inspires other people.
Community colleges: two-year schools that offer associate's degrees.
Contacts: people you can get in touch with, either in person or by phone or e-mail.
Embraced: accepted.
Financing: getting money to pay for something.
Genetic: relating to the passing of inherited traits from parent to child.
Grants: money given by governments and budinesses to organizations or individuals for a specific purpose.
Industry: all of the businesses that sell the same product or service.
Integrity: honesty and trustworthiness.
Invest: to give or spend money in expectation of receiving more money back.
Loans: money given by the banks or the government, which must be paid back.
Manage: to direct or organize.

Media: means of mass communication, such as television, newspapers, and magazines.
Mentor: someone who advises and guides a younger or less experienced person.
Nonprofit: an organization that uses the money it makes to further a social cause.
Passion: an intense love or excitement about something.
Profits: the money that a business makes after it accounts for expenses.
Rioting: a public and often violent gathering in reaction to an event or idea.
Seed funding: money given to a business when it is just starting out.
Stereotyped: assumed to have certain characteristics because of a social identity such as race, age, gender, or religion.
Trade shows: gatherings of similar businesses where they can display their products or services.
Ventures: risky businesses.

Index

adults 31, 33–34, 47
Archer, Leanna 44, 46

Bradshaw, Maddie 48
business plan 7, 17–18

class 33, 35, 55
creativity 22, 55

Damacela, Zoe 53

experience 28–29, 32–36

Food From the 'Hood 55–59

grants 17, 50

Horwitz, Adam 40

ideas 7, 13, 15, 17, 19, 21, 24, 26–28, 31–35, 40, 43
Internet 43–44
invest 17

leadership 25, 46, 59

money 12–15, 17–19, 23, 25, 29, 32–33, 40, 43, 46, 49–50, 53, 55–59

passion 21, 24, 44, 59, 62
planning 17
problems 13, 16, 19, 22–24, 29, 34, 46, 56

qualities 22, 28

risk 11–13, 16, 28, 55

Samar, Anshul 49
school 9, 11, 29, 31, 33, 35, 43, 46, 53, 56–58
self-confidence 26–27
social entrepreneur 12, 46
studies 22

training 31, 41

About the Author and Consultant

C.F. Earl is a writer living and working in Binghamton, New York. Earl writes mostly on social and historical topics, including health, the military, and finances.

Brigitte Madrian is the Aetna Professor of Public Policy and Corporate Management at the Harvard Kennedy School. Before coming to Harvard in 2006, she was on the faculty at the University of Pennsylvania Wharton School (2003–2006), the University of Chicago Graduate School of Business (1995–2003) and the Harvard University Economics Department (1993–1995). She is also a research associate and co-director of the Household Finance working group at the National Bureau of Economic Research. Dr. Madrian received her PhD in economics from the Massachusetts Institute of Technology and studied economics as an undergraduate at Brigham Young University. She is the recipient of the National Academy of Social Insurance Dissertation Prize (first place, 1994) and a two-time recipient of the TIAA-CREF Paul A. Samuelson Award for Scholarly Research on Lifelong Financial Security (2002 and 2011).

Picture Credits

p. 10: Rimma Zaytseva (Dreamstime Stock Photos); p. 12: Maurice Jordan De Souza Coelho (Dreamstime); p. 15: Jason Stitt (Dreamstime); p. 16: Stitt; p. 20: Dreamstime Agency; p. 25: Alphaspirit; p. 30: Piotr Marcinski (Dreamstime); p. 34: Branislav Ostojic (Dreamstime); p. 36: EPA; p. 38: Phil Date (Dreamstime); p. 40: Millionaire at Twenty-Four; pp. 41, 42: Dude, I Hate My Job; p. 45: Alfred Edmond Jr.; p. 47: US Navy; p. 48: M3 Girl Designs; p. 51: Alchemist Empire; p. 52: Network for Teaching Enterprize; p. 54: Seventeen Magazine; p. 56: Lamiot; p. 58: Albaum